Make Jungle animals

Gillian Chapman

Miles Kelly

First published in 2013 by Miles Kelly Publishing Ltd
Harding's Barn, Bardfield End Green, Thaxted, Essex, CM6 3PX, UK

2 4 6 8 10 9 7 5 3 1

Author, illustrator and model maker Gillian Chapman
Publishing Director Belinda Gallagher
Creative Director Jo Cowan
Managing Editor Amanda Askew
Senior Editor Sarah Parkin
Designer Joe Jones
Photographer Alex Bibby
Production Manager Elizabeth Collins
Reprographics Stephan Davis, Thom Allaway, Jenni Hunt

ISBN 978-1-78209-207-0

Printed in China

British Library Cataloguing-in-Publication Data
A catalogue record for this book is available from the British Library

Acknowledgements

Poster: Pete Oxford/Minden Pictures/FLPA (South American yellow-footed tortoise),
Jurgen & Christine Sohns/FLPA (scarlet macaw), Piotr Naskrecki/Minden Pictures/FLPA (leaf-cutter ant),
Nick Garbutt/Nature Picture Library (jewelled chameleon). All other images courtesy of Shutterstock –
Eric Isselee, Andreas Gradin, paulrommer, LeonP, worldswildlifewonders, tratong, Audrey Snider-Bell,
Jeremy Reddington, Cosmin Manci, Smit, Itinerant Lens

Every effort has been made to acknowledge the source and copyright holder of each picture.
Miles Kelly Publishing apologises for any unintentional errors or omissions.

Made with paper from a sustainable forest

www.mileskelly.net
info@mileskelly.net

Important notice
The publisher and author cannot be held
responsible for any injuries, damage or loss
resulting from the use or misuse of any of the
information in this book.

Contents

Plus...

The poster shows you what jungle animals look like in real life.

Add the colourful eye stickers to your crafts.

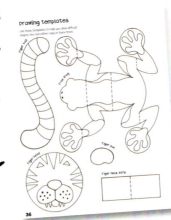

The templates will help you draw the shapes needed for some of the projects.

How to use this book

Do you like making things? Are you an animal lover?

Then you'll love the 15 fun projects in this book. Read the instructions carefully and ask an adult if you need help.

Symbols

🖐 This tells you if you need to ask an adult for help.

⏱ This tells you how long the project will take, once you have collected the equipment.

✂ This tells you how difficult the project is. ★ is the easiest and ★★★ is the most difficult.

Before you start!

- Clear a surface to work on and cover it with newspaper.
- Wear an apron or old t-shirt to protect your clothing.
- Gather all the equipment you need.

You will need

The equipment should be easy to find, around the house or from a craft store. Always ask before using materials from home.

Iguana

Make a colourful lizard for a special puppet show!

🖐 Some help needed

⏱ 30 minutes, plus drying time

✂ ★★

YOU WILL NEED

- Acrylic paint – green
- Card – green (A4)
- Eye sticker provided
- Felt pen – black
- Palette
- Pen (old)
- Pencil (sharp)
- Scissors
- 3 split pins
- Stick (20 cm)
- String – green
- Toothbrush (old)

1 Put paint on the toothbrush and rub it up and down the pen

Use the toothbrush and pen to splatter green paint on two pieces of green card. Leave to dry.

2

Using the templates, draw the iguana body, head and legs on the splatter-painted card. Cut them out.

3 You could use a hole punch to make the holes

Using a sharp pencil, make holes in the head, body and legs. Draw the mouth and nostril with the black felt pen. Add the eye sticker.

4 Make each hole one by one

Position the head and legs on the body. Push the sharp pencil through the holes to make new holes in the body.

Notes for helpers

• Children will need supervision for some of the projects, usually because they require the use of scissors, or preparation beforehand. These projects are marked with 'Help needed'.

• Read the instructions together before starting and help to gather the equipment.

• Help children with the 'Also make...' projects, or search the Internet for more ideas. There are hundreds of craft websites to choose from.

Numbered stages

Each stage of the project is numbered and illustrated. Follow the stages in the order shown to complete the project.

make each piece of string the same length

Attach the head and legs to the body with split pins, pushing them through the holes and opening them at the back.

Thread string through the holes in the body and head. Tie the string around the stick.

Finished project photo

At the end of each project, the photo shows what your craft should look like.

Don't worry if it looks a bit different. Making things is about having fun!

Wiggle the stick between your fingers to make the iguana move!

Also make... a chameleon

Follow the same steps, but draw a chameleon shape and use blue, orange and green paints.

Also make...

With just a few simple changes, you can make fun variations of some crafts.

31

5

Tree frog

Give a friend a 'hoppy' birthday with a pop-out card!

 Some help needed

40 minutes

★★

YOU WILL NEED

- Acrylic paint – blue, orange, yellow
- Card – thin light green, thin dark green (A4)
- Eye stickers provided
- Glue stick
- Paintbrush
- Paper – assorted green
- Pencil
- Scissors

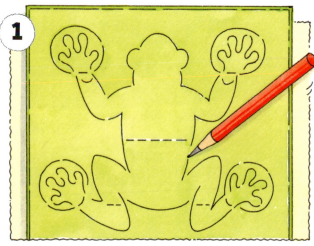

1 Using the template, draw the frog outline on the light-green card.

2 Cut out. Make folds along the dotted lines.

3 Draw markings on the body and paint them blue and yellow. Paint the feet orange. Add the eye stickers.

4 Fold the dark-green card in half. Cut out leaf shapes from the green paper and glue them to the inside and front of the green card.

Make your leaves different sizes

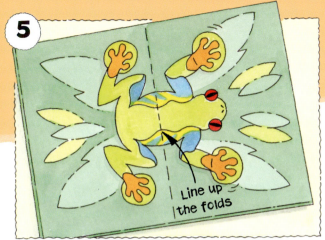

5

Line up the folds

Position the frog on the inside of the card by lining up the centre folds.

6

Hold the frog in place and glue the feet to the card.

RIBBIT! RIBBIT!

open the card and the frog will jump out!

write a greeting on the outside of the card

HAPPY

BIRTHDAY

Lemur

Put on a lemur show with these fantastic finger puppets!

Help not needed

30 minutes

★

YOU WILL NEED

- Coloured pencil – grey
- Eye stickers provided
- Felt pen – black
- Glue stick
- Paper – thick grey (A4), thick white (A4)
- Paperclip
- Pencil
- Plate (about 15 cm in diameter)
- Scissors

1

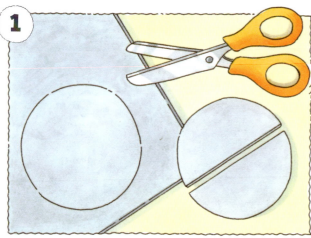

Draw around the plate on grey paper. Cut out the circle, then cut it in half.

2

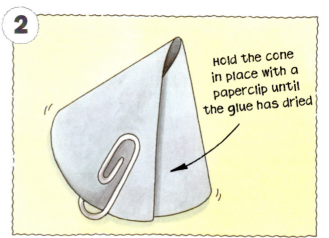

Hold the cone in place with a paperclip until the glue has dried

Bend one half into a cone shape. Glue the edges together.

3

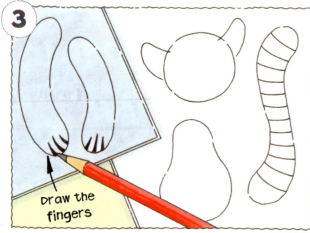

Draw the fingers

Using the templates, draw the head, tail and body patch on white paper. Draw the arms on grey paper. Cut them out.

4

Colour the ears, eyes and nose patch grey. Add grey shading around the body patch. Draw the mouth and nostrils with black felt pen. Add the eye stickers.

5

colour in the tail on both sides

Colour in the tail stripes with black felt pen.

6

Glue the head, arms, body patch and tail to the cone. Leave to dry.

Also make... lots of lemurs with different facial expressions to make your show great!

put the arms in different positions

Parrot

Keep your notepad handy with a colourful holder!

 Some help needed

40 minutes

★★

YOU WILL NEED

- Card – red (A4)
- Eye sticker provided
- Glue stick
- Paper – black, blue, red, white, yellow
- Pencil (sharp)
- Scissors
- Sticky notepad (square, 7.5 cm)
- String

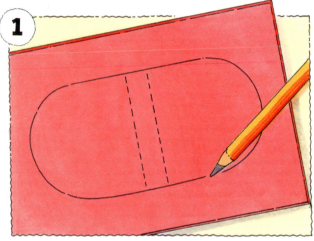

1 Using the template, draw the parrot's body shape on the red card.

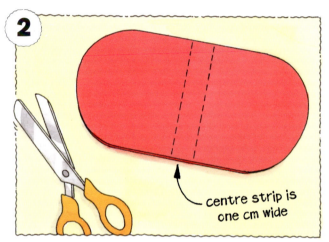

2 centre strip is one cm wide

Cut out the body shape and fold along the dotted lines.

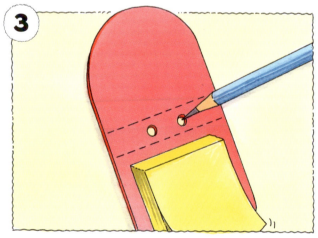

3 Make two holes in the centre strip with a sharp pencil. Glue the notepad to the inside.

4 Thread the string through the holes and knot the ends together.

5

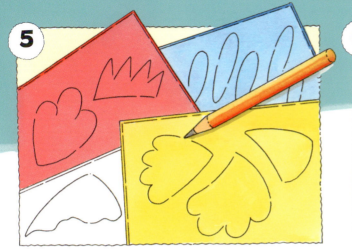

Using the templates, draw the beak on white and black paper, and feather shapes on the red, yellow and blue paper. Cut them out.

6

Glue the feathers and beak to the inside and outside of the front flap (as shown). Add the eye sticker.

Use the string to hang up your notepad

SQUAWK!

Also make... a toucan
Follow the same steps, but use different-coloured card and paper.

Tarantula

Make a creepy crawly badge to scare your friends!

Some help needed

30 minutes

★★

YOU WILL NEED

- 8 beads – red
- Eye stickers provided
- Felt – brown, orange
- Glue brush
- Paper – scrap
- Pins
- 5 pipe cleaners – brown
- PVA glue
- Safety pin
- Scissors
- Sewing needle
- Thread – brown

1 Cut out an oval from a piece of paper. Pin it to the orange felt. Cut around it to make two felt oval shapes. Repeat with a smaller oval.

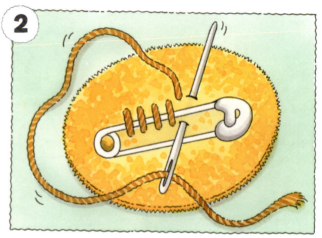

2 Sew the safety pin to a larger felt oval. Make sure the safety pin can be opened and closed.

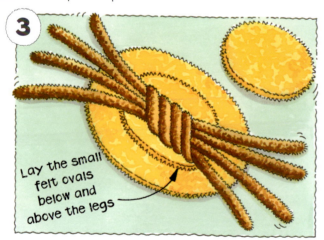

3 Lay the small felt ovals below and above the legs

To make the legs, hold four pipe cleaners together and wrap another pipe cleaner around the middle. Lay them across the second large felt oval.

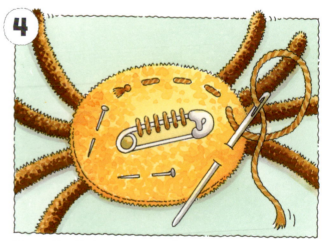

4 Place the felt with the safety pin on top. Pin the two large felt pieces together, and then sew them together.

5 Push the beads down the pipe cleaners a little

Add glue to the ends of each pipe cleaner leg and push the beads onto them. Leave to dry.

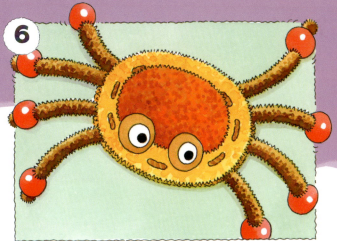

6

Cut out a small oval from brown felt and glue it to the top of the body. Add the eye stickers.

Pin the badges to your jacket or school bag

The body patch can be any colour you like

Also make... different-coloured tarantulas to give to all of your friends!

snake

Hang some springy snakes around your bedroom!

Some help needed

30 minutes

★★

YOU WILL NEED

- Acrylic paint – white
- Card – thin green (A4), dark green, pink
- Eye stickers provided
- Felt pen – black
- Glue stick
- Paintbrush
- Pencil
- Scissors
- Sewing needle
- Thread – green

Using the template, draw the coiled snake shape on the green card.

Cut out the snake, carefully following the spiral of the snake's body.

Paint white markings along the snake's body.

Draw several leaves of different shapes and sizes on the dark-green card. Cut them out.

5

Cut out a long forked tongue from the pink card and glue it to the head. Draw the nostrils and mouth with black felt pen. Add the eye stickers.

6

Tie a knot in the end of the thread and push the threaded needle through the snake's head. Tie a knot. Repeat for all of the leaf shapes.

Also make... lots of snakes, using different-coloured card, to hang all around your home!

HISSSS! HISSSS!

Hang up your snake and watch it twist round and round

Tiger

Keep your savings safe with this toothy tiger!

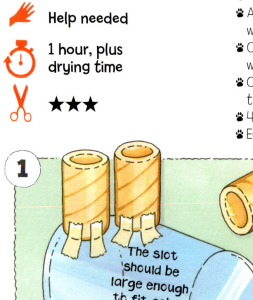

Help needed

1 hour, plus drying time

★★★

YOU WILL NEED

- Acrylic paint – black, orange, white
- Card – brown, dark orange, white
- Card tube with lid (eg biscuit tube, 12 cm long)
- 4 card tubes (6 cm x 3 cm)
- Eye stickers provided
- Felt pen – black
- Glue brush
- Masking tape
- Newspaper
- Paintbrush
- Pencil
- PVA glue
- Scissors

1

The slot should be large enough to fit coins through

Before you start, ask an adult to cut a slot in the side of the large tube. Tape the four card tubes on the opposite side to the slot.

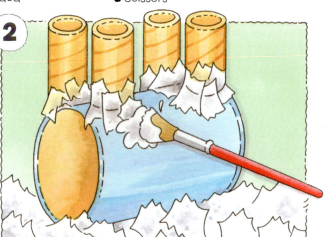

2

Glue small pieces of newspaper all over the body and legs. Don't cover the slot or the lid. Leave to dry.

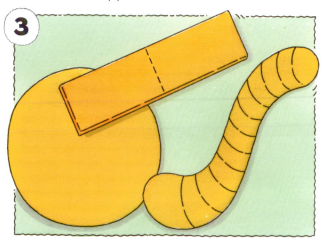

3

Using the templates, draw the head, neck strip, ears, mouth and tail on the dark-orange card. Draw the nose on brown card. Draw teeth on white card. Cut them out.

4

Glue the ears, mouth, nose and teeth to the head. Draw the stripes, eyebrows and spots with black felt pen. Add the eye stickers.

5

Paint the body and legs orange and white. Leave to dry. Paint black stripes.

6

Paint on both sides

Paint black stripes on the tail. Paint the tip white. Glue the tail to the tube lid.

7

Fold the neck strip in half and glue it to the body. Glue the head to the neck.

Get coins out by removing the lid

Insert coins through the slot

SNARL!

Ant

Hold up notes and photos with brilliant bug magnets!

Help not needed

20 minutes

★

YOU WILL NEED
- Card – thin green
- Felt pen – red
- Foam – green
- Glue stick
- Magnet
- Paper – scrap
- Pencil
- Scissors

1

Using the template, draw a leaf shape on a piece of paper. Cut it out. Cut around it to make a leaf-shaped base from the green foam.

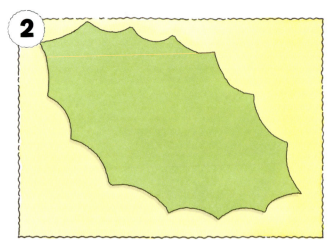

2

Using the template, draw a jagged leaf shape on the green card. Cut it out.

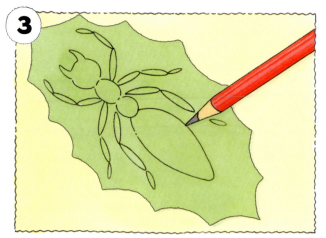

3

Using the template, draw the outline of the ant on the card leaf.

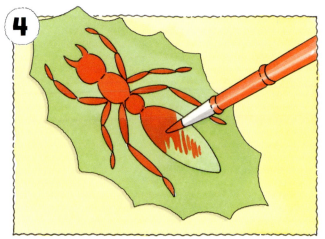

4

Colour in the ant using the red felt pen.

5

Glue the card leaf onto the foam leaf.

6

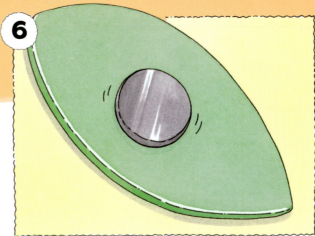

Glue the magnet to the back of the foam leaf.

Decorate your fridge or radiator with swarms of ants!

Make your ants lots of different colours

Also make... a Hercules beetle
Follow the same steps, but draw a beetle shape instead.

caiman

Make a super snappy card for any special occasion!

 Some help needed

40 minutes

★★

YOU WILL NEED
- Card – thin blue (A4), white
- Coloured paper
- Eye sticker provided
- Felt pens
- Glue stick
- Pencil (sharp)
- Ruler
- Scissors
- Split pin

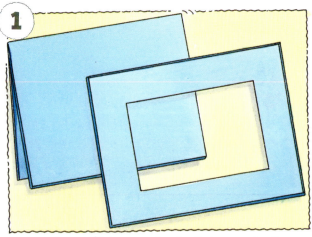

1 Cut a piece of blue card in half. On one half, draw a frame and cut out the centre. Fold another piece of blue card in half.

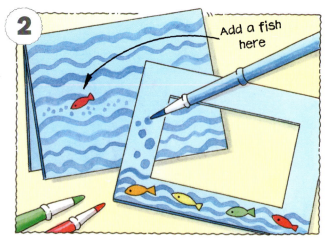

2 Add a fish here

On the front of the folded card and the frame, draw waves with blue felt pen. Cut out fish from coloured paper and glue to both pieces.

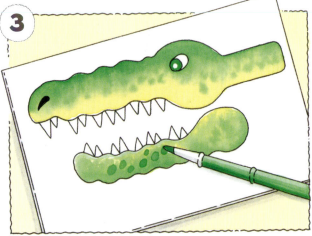

3 Using the templates, draw the jaws on white card. Colour them in with the felt pens. Cut them out. Add an eye sticker.

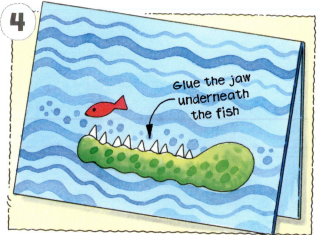

4 Glue the jaw underneath the fish

Glue the lower jaw to the front of the card.

5

check where the holes should go before making them

Using a sharp pencil, make a small hole in the frame and the upper jaw. Attach the upper jaw to the back of the frame with the split pin.

6

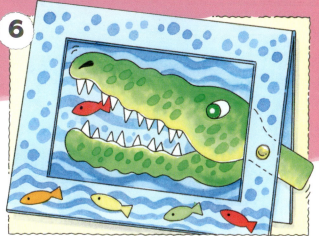

Glue the other three sides of the frame to the front of the folded card. Leave to dry.

SNAP! SNAP!

Move the lever up and down to see the caiman eat the fish!

write a message inside the card

Happy Birthday

butterfly

Decorate your windows with beautiful fluttery butterflies!

Help not needed

20 minutes

★

YOU WILL NEED
- 2 beads – pink (1 cm)
- Button (about 1.2 cm)
- Glue brush
- Paper – pink, purple
- Pencil
- Pipe cleaner – pink (30 cm long)
- PVA glue
- Scissors
- Suction cap (2 cm diameter)

1 Fold the pink paper in half. Using the template, draw half a butterfly along the folded edge. Cut it out.

2 Using the template, draw the wing patterns on the pink and purple paper. Cut them out and glue to the butterfly.

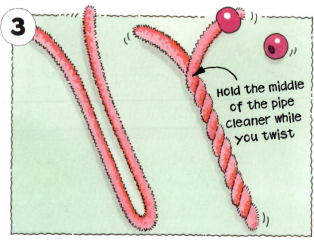

3 *Hold the middle of the pipe cleaner while you twist*

To make the body, fold the pipe cleaner in half, then twist together. Leave some untwisted. Glue the beads onto the ends.

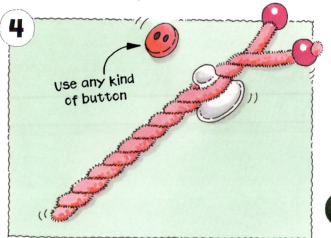

4 *Use any kind of button*

Add glue to the back of the suction cap and twist the pipe cleaner around it. Glue the button to the back of the cap. Leave to dry.

5

Glue the body along the centre of the wings. Leave to dry.

6

wet the suction cap slightly if it won't stick

Carefully push the suction cap onto your bedroom window.

FLUTTER!

you could use glittery card to make your butterfly sparkle

FLUTTER!

Orang-utan

Keep your pens and pencils inside a bright holder!

Some help needed

1 hour, plus
drying time

★★

YOU WILL NEED

- Acrylic paint – brown, orange
- Card tube (eg biscuit tube, 12 cm x 7 cm)
- Coloured pencils – brown, orange
- Eye stickers provided
- Felt pen – black
- Glue stick
- Paintbrush
- Palette (for mixing paints)
- Paper – brown strip (10 cm x 4 cm), green, grey, orange
- Pencil
- Scissors

1

Your palette could be an old plate

Mix orange and brown paint together in the palette. Paint the card tube and leave to dry.

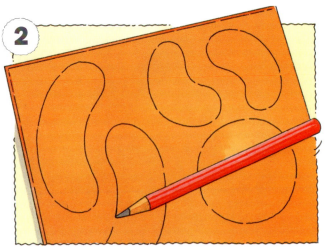

2

Using the templates, draw the head, arms and legs on the orange paper. Cut them out.

3

Glue down the small oval first

Using the templates, draw two oval shapes on the grey paper. Cut them out and glue them to the head.

4

Add shading to the head with the orange and brown coloured pencils. Draw the eyebrows, nostrils and mouth with the black felt pen. Add the eye stickers.

5

Draw the fingers and toes with black felt pen

Add shading to the arms and legs with the coloured pencils. Glue the head, arms and legs to the body.

6

Roll the strip of brown paper to make a branch. Cut out leaf shapes from the green paper and glue them to the branch. Tuck it under the orang-utan's arm.

Also make...
a set of ape or monkey holders, each using different-coloured paints and paper.

Keep your pens and pencils tidy

Sloth

Give your friends and family rocking greetings cards!

Some help needed

40 minutes

★★

YOU WILL NEED

- Acrylic paint – green
- Card – thin brown, grey (A5)
- Coloured pencils – black, brown, grey
- Eye stickers provided
- Felt pen – black
- Glue stick
- Paintbrush
- Paper – green
- 2 paperclips
- Paper plate, or round piece of card (19 cm diameter)
- Pencil
- Scissors
- Split pin

1

Keep the plate folded with paperclips

Fold the paper plate and paint it green. Cut a strip of leaves from the green paper and glue it to the folded edge of the plate.

2

Using the templates, draw the sloth's body and head on grey card. Draw a branch on brown card. Cut them out.

3

Add shading to the sloth's body using the grey pencil. Shade along the bottom of the branch with the brown pencil.

4

Add the eye stickers

Add shading around the edge of the face and eyes using the black pencil. Draw the nose, mouth and spots with the black felt pen.

5 Attach the head to the body by pushing the split pin through the nose. Glue the sloth's feet to the branch.

6 Make sure you don't glue it on too low down

Glue the branch and sloth's body to the plate. Draw the claws with the black felt pen.

write your message inside or along the branch

Push down on the branch to make the sloth rock

Thank you

Tapir

Keep your books tidy with this long-nosed bookend!

Help needed

1 hour, plus
drying time

★★★

YOU WILL NEED

- Acrylic paint – black, white
- Card – thick, scrap
- 4 card tubes (5 cm x 2.5 cm)
- Eye stickers provided
- Glue brush
- Masking tape
- Newspaper
- Paintbrush
- Paper towel
- Pebble (large)
- PVA glue
- Scissors

1

To make the body, cover the pebble with layers of newspaper. Tape it tightly in place with masking tape.

2

Tape the card tubes to the body. Glue small pieces of newspaper to the joins. Leave to dry.

3

Cut out two card ears and tape them to the front of the body.

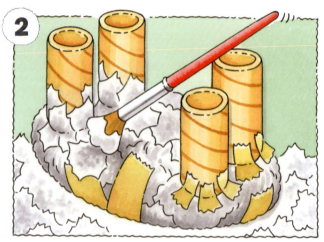

4

Glue small pieces of paper towel all over the body, legs and ears. Leave to dry.

5

Twist a piece of paper towel for the tail and snout. Glue them in place. Leave to dry.

6

Paint the tapir black and white. Paint the mouth, toes and ear tips white. Add the eye stickers.

Make two tapirs to hold up each end of your row of books

Give your tapir a big grin

Iguana

Make a colourful lizard for a special puppet show!

 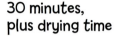

Some help needed

30 minutes, plus drying time

★★

YOU WILL NEED

- Acrylic paint – green
- Card – green (A4)
- Eye sticker provided
- Felt pen – black
- Palette
- Pen (old)
- Pencil (sharp)

- Scissors
- 3 split pins
- Stick (20 cm)
- String – green
- Toothbrush (old)

1

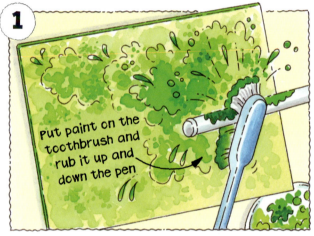

Put paint on the toothbrush and rub it up and down the pen

Use the toothbrush and pen to splatter green paint on two pieces of green card. Leave to dry.

2

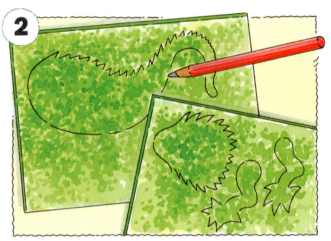

Using the templates, draw the iguana body, head and legs on the splatter-painted card. Cut them out.

3

you could use a hole punch to make the holes

Using a sharp pencil, make holes in the head, body and legs. Draw the mouth and nostril with the black felt pen. Add the eye sticker.

4

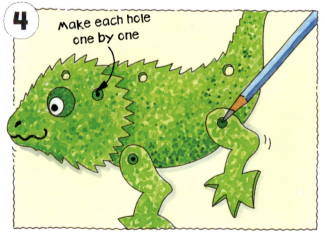

make each hole one by one

Position the head and legs on the body. Push the sharp pencil through the holes to make new holes in the body.

5

Attach the head and legs to the body with split pins, pushing them through the holes and opening them at the back.

6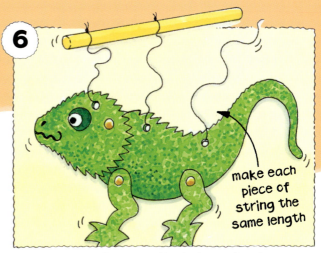

make each piece of string the same length

Thread string through the holes in the body and head. Tie the string around the stick.

wiggle the stick between your fingers to make the iguana move!

Also make... a chameleon
Follow the same steps, but draw a chameleon shape and use blue, orange and green paints.

Eagle

Impress your friends with this magnificent mask!

Some help needed

30 minutes

★

YOU WILL NEED
- Card – thin assorted grey (A4)
- Elastic (thin, 35 cm)
- Felt pen – black
- Glue stick
- Pencil (sharp)
- Scissors

1

Draw the mask shape on a shade of grey card. Draw the beak and feathers of different sizes on shades of grey card. Cut them out.

2

Make the holes eye shaped

Put the mask against your face and ask an adult to mark where your eyes are. Cut out two eye holes.

3

Glue the small feathers to the front of the mask. Leave to dry.

4

Turn over the mask and glue the large feathers to the back. They can overlap each other. Leave to dry.

5

Add glue to the edges of the beak

Bend the beak shape along the dotted line and glue it to the front of the mask. Draw the nostrils and eyelids using the black felt pen.

6

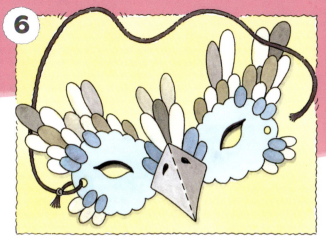

Make a small hole in each side of the mask using a sharp pencil. Thread the elastic through the holes and tie it in place.

Also make... other bird masks using different-coloured card and different-shaped feathers.

wear your mask to look like a fierce eagle

Tortoise

Make a treasure box to keep your trinkets safe!

Help needed

1.5 hours, plus drying time

★★★

YOU WILL NEED

- Acrylic paint – dark brown, light brown, yellow
- Card (thick)
- Card box (round, 11 cm diameter)
- Eye stickers provided
- Felt pen – black
- Glue brush
- Masking tape
- Paintbrush
- Palette (old plate)
- Paper towel
- Pencil
- Polystyrene craft ball (5 cm in diameter)
- PVA glue
- Scissors

1 Using the templates, draw the legs, tail and neck on the card. Cut them out and glue them to the base of the box. Leave to dry.

2 Make a pad of paper towel and tape it to the top of the lid. This is the domed shell.

you could use a cheese triangle box

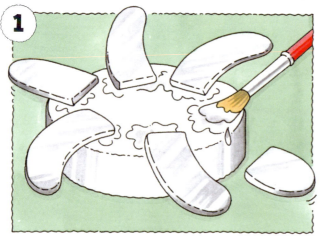

3 Glue the polystyrene ball to the neck. Cover the head, legs and tail with small pieces of glued paper towel.

4 Using the templates, draw the shell shapes on thick card. Cut them out and glue to the lid.

5

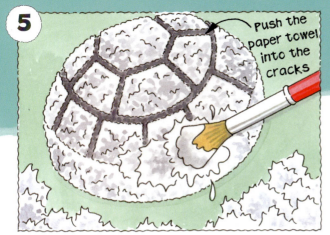

Push the paper towel into the cracks

Cover the shell with a layer of glued paper towel. Leave to dry.

6

Paint the tortoise yellow and light brown. Dab dark-brown paint over the body and in between the shell shapes. Draw the nostrils and mouth with the black felt pen. Add the eye stickers.

Also make...
other tortoises using different-coloured paints and give them to your friends!

store your treasures inside the tortoise's body

Drawing templates

Use these templates to help you draw difficult shapes. You can either copy or trace them.

Tiger tail

Tree frog

Tiger head

Tiger ear

Tiger neck strip

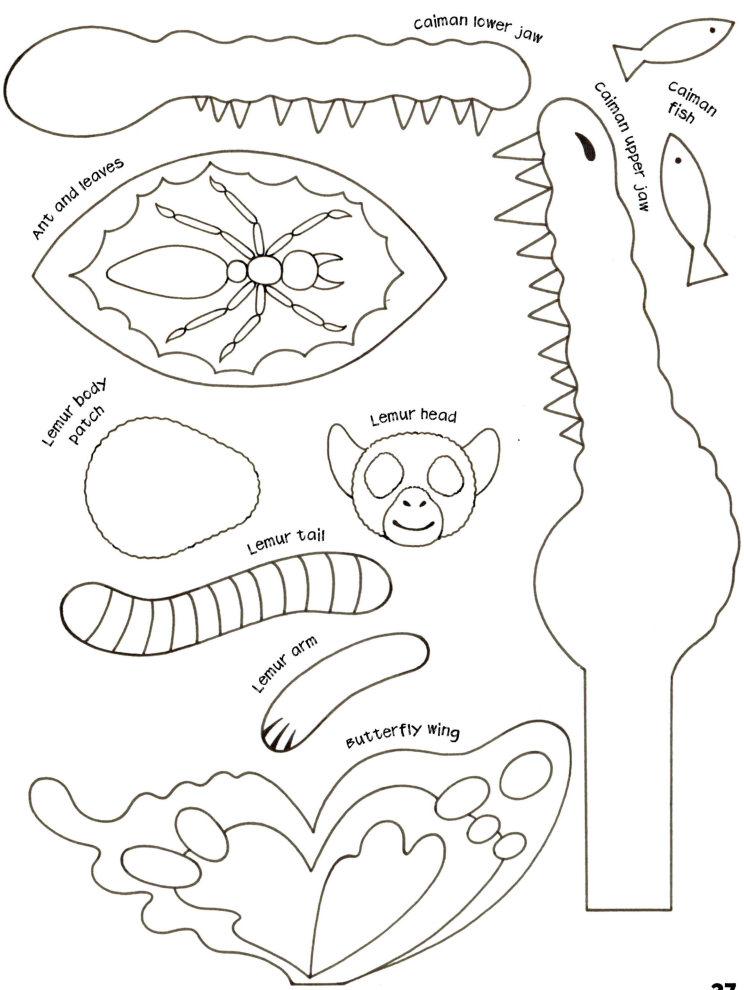

caiman lower jaw

Caiman fish

caiman upper jaw

Ant and leaves

Lemur body patch

Lemur head

Lemur tail

Lemur arm

Butterfly wing

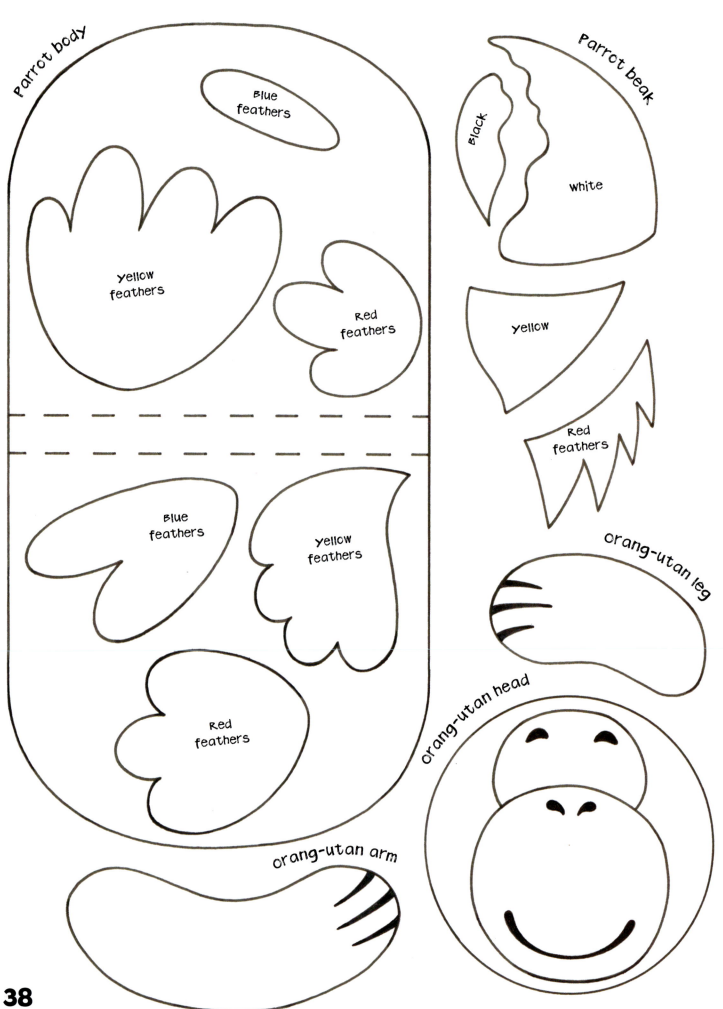

Parrot body

Blue
feathers

Yellow
feathers

Red
feathers

Blue
feathers

Yellow
feathers

Red
feathers

Parrot beak

Black

white

Yellow

Red
feathers

orang-utan leg

orang-utan head

orang-utan arm

38

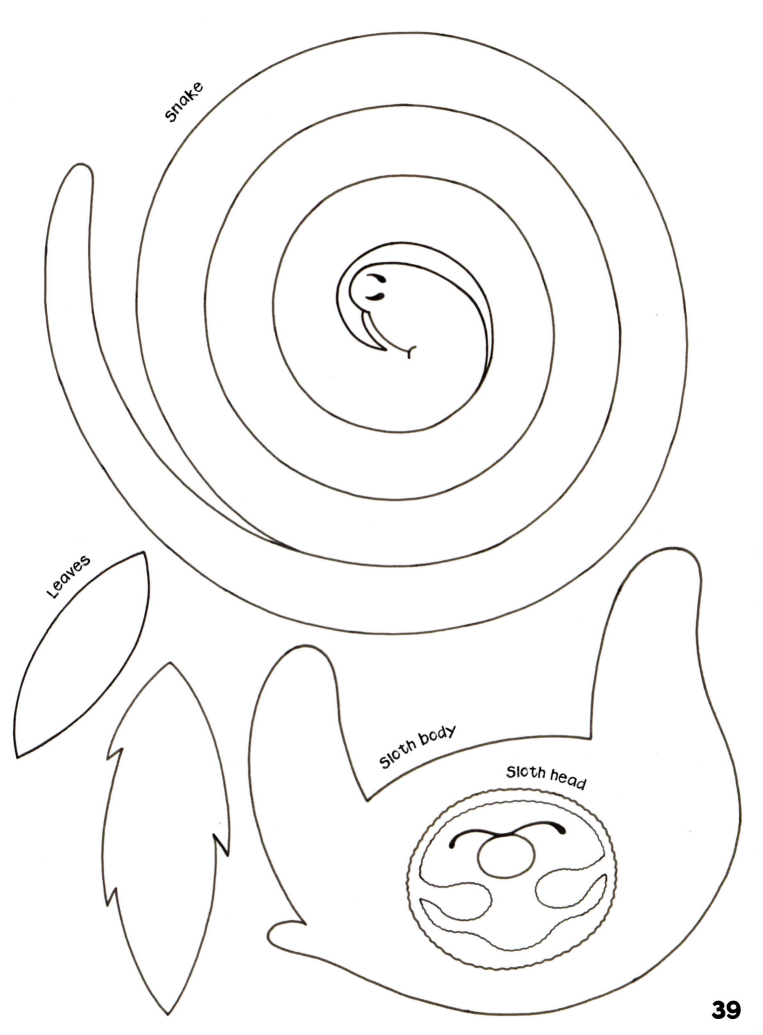

Snake

Leaves

Sloth body

Sloth head

39

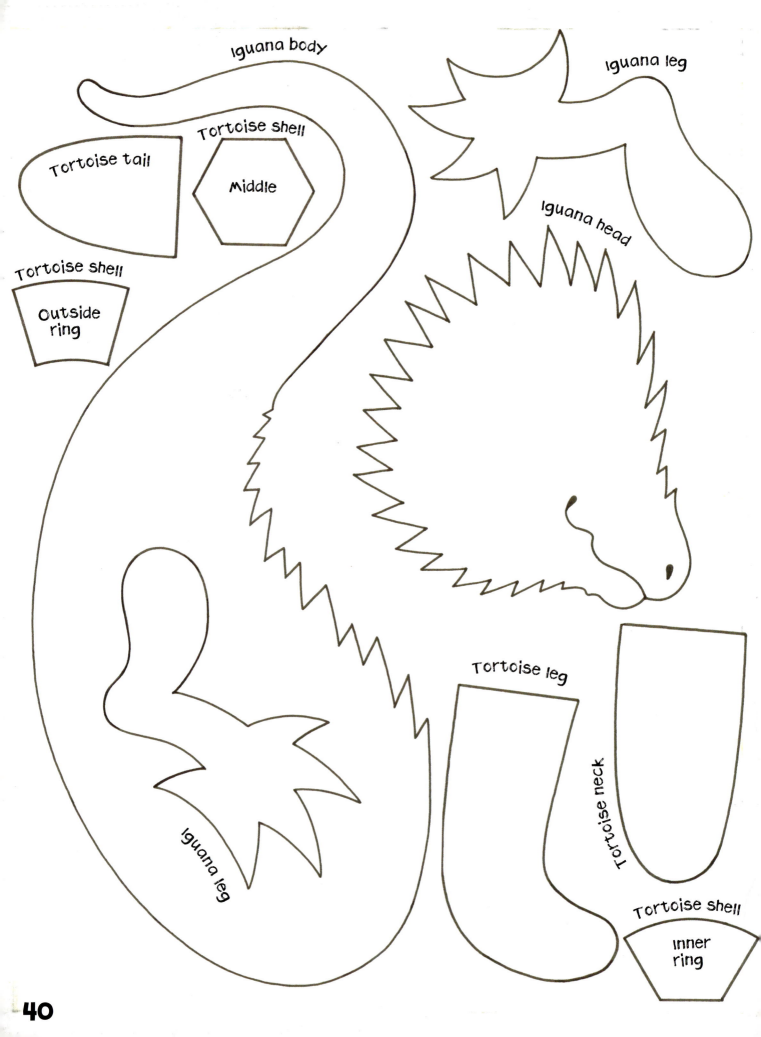

Iguana body

Iguana leg

Tortoise tail

Tortoise shell

Middle

Iguana head

Tortoise shell

Outside ring

Tortoise leg

Tortoise neck

Iguana leg

Tortoise shell

Inner ring

40